Dreaming in Spices

Suchismita Dutta

BookLeaf Publishing

India | USA | UK

Presentation by *BookLeaf Publishing*

Web: www.bookleafpub.com

E-mail: info@bookleafpub.com

ISBN: 9789360940614

First edition 2024

*To Rahul and Amu. May we keep sharing
the flavors of life.*

Panch Phoron, the five-spice blend

Fenugreek seeds, nigella seeds, cumin seeds,
mustard and fennel;
I made a list and walked into the Indian grocery
store
in Miami.

I was now an immigrant, a PhD student but an
immigrant nonetheless
in the United States
For someone who has never cooked before
this was an adventure to find home
or the aroma of home

Panch phoron or the five-spice blend
fried in a bit of mustard oil
chopped potatoes added to the mix
a touch of salt and sugar and may be
one dried red chili
a white gooey delicious potato curry
"Shada aloor torkari," as we call it in Bengali

What if I didn't find all the ingredients
in Mr. Khan's grocery store?
Getting the five ingredients was essential

for this was an adventure to find home
or the aroma of home

With one happy heart
I carried the spices, tightly packed in a plastic
bag
dangling on the right handlebar of my bike
I had begun my adventure to find home
in the kitchen of an old apartment
across the university

That night
I shared the potato curry with my two
roommates
one from Brazil, one from England

the five-spice blend brought three countries
closer than they could ever be.

So much of everything

I wonder often
why do I feel so much
of everything,
happiness, grief, jealousy, arrogance
the boundless love of motherly nurture
gently cradling the baby in a warm embrace
like a talisman warding off evil

I wonder often
why does this jealousy grow on me
like a purple serpent wrapped around my limbs
making it difficult to move or blink
as if I am the evil casting a black eye
on the successes I could never have

I wonder often
why does this anger feel so warm
it bubbles and boils inside
causing a fever that wouldn't subside
even after taking the strongest dose of
medication
as if I could burn everything around
like the wildfires of California
one spark and half the forest turns to ash

I wonder often
why does my grief feel endless
like the river Ganges in Benares
only less forgiving and far less calming
devoid of the bright oil lamps of worship
it ebbs and flows and pains
a tumor malignant enough to kill, but doesn't

I wonder often
why my love for you reaches the heights
of sacrifices, compromises and passions
like I could keep touching you from dawn to
dusk
especially on long summer days
when the sun never sets

As I wonder
I feel more, the heights and depths
Oh, the joy of being able to feel so much
the abundance, the lack, the losses and gains
the scented happiness of lavender fields
the wound from a sharp cut that throbs and pains

as I wonder
as I wander

Mr. Khan's Grocery in Miami

5

Cling, ding, ding

The doorbell rang every time someone entered
Mr. Khan's Grocery
about 250 sq ft, packed with spices, Indian and
Pakistani snacks, biscuits
sweets, pickles, microwavable desi meals
3 minutes in 350 degrees
and you have home on a plate

And then there was a concoction of aromas
of samosas, tamarind and cilantro chutney,
masala chai with extra cardamom
the beef kabab rolls
specially made by Mrs. Khan in a curtained back
kitchen
where no one was allowed
"Assalam walikum, did you find everything
okay?"
-"Yes, Mr. Khan. Thank you."

Cling, ding, ding

Dreaming in spices

I dream in spices as I think of home
A careful mix of turmeric and red chili powder
a few pinches of cumin and coriander
a generous dollop of ginger and garlic paste
as the sizzle of oil spreads through my mind
I think of home

Why did I think our kitchen was too small?
like a little alleyway
but it fit all my mother's spices, oils, herbs, and
even
a mini kitchen garden on the window pane
the size didn't matter because it held
everything that we needed to feel nourished

I dream in spices when I think of home
spices that coat the vegetables and meat
the smoke from the kadhai rises into a
warm embrace on Sunday afternoons
like a genie emerging from a slow coil of smoke
I can hear my mother asking me to check the salt
in her chicken curry, a Sunday special.
My tastebuds and my stomach grin ear to ear
and then we all collapse into the comforting
crevasses
of a Sunday siesta

Dry roast

The skillet makes love
to the hasty grains of coriander
the seeds play hard to get
flirting around the rounded edges
until they succumb to a warm brown color
and a nutty aroma

I call a love like this
the perfect dry roast.

Mother tongue

I think in Bengali
before I speak in English.
Sometimes you can taste a pinch of Hindi
if we get too intimate.

Sometimes the right words don't come through
when I am thinking in English,
then my mother tongue comes to the rescue.
Here is the alternative word in Bangla
translate it into English and voila!

Thank God, I think in Bengali
When I speak in English.

Maa's love

My mother's love was always strange
never too touchy feely yet profound
like the mountains strong and tall that keep
giving
a bit like water, all sustaining
The kisses were few and the hugs were less
but on nights I had fever,
she stayed awake to nurse me back to health
and she prayed and prayed and prayed,
that if anything bad were to happen,
it should pass her first
until the danger was eliminated
and we were safe.

Perhaps that's why we lost her so soon.

Masala chai

A cold December morning in Delhi
the "thunk thunk" of the mortar and pestle
grinding bits of ginger and pods of cardamom;
the chai seller adds the spice
to the bubbling milk, tea and water with rapt
attention
then he carefully strains and pours
a simmering liquid of golden joy
piping hot cups of masala chai.

I tightly hold my lover's hand
partly to keep my hands warm
and partly to cling on to the freezing, foggy
morning
that enters my body with each sip I take.

Masala chai is very forgiving
a gentle blow on the earthen cup,
the smoke separates from the hot tea
ready to be consumed.
A magic potion that heals and calms
the feverish mind, the broken heart.

At the airport

"I will be back next summer."
said I, as I hugged Maa and Baba
They wiped their tears
And I, mine

Leaving behind the smell of spices,
the warmth of chai,
the big bougainvillea tree engulfing half our
balcony
in a tight pink embrace
the big poster of Shah Rukh Khan in my study
room
"The best Bollywood Hero!" written with a
sparkly marker
Tears of separation
They wiped theirs
And I, mine

The first university graduate in the family
Baba's pride and Maa's little girl
It will be a wait of another year
They wiped their tears
And I, mine

Next Summer

February
It's a virus. Just like the common cold
"Don't worry, Maa. This is temporary.
Yes, by summer everything will be fine."
The summer sun will heal
it will kill the virus, doctors say
that summer passed
that winter too

Seasons disappeared into a void
along with thoughts of homecoming
"I will be back next summer, Maa"
The summer sun will heal
it will kill the virus, scientists say
that summer passed
that winter too.

Departures

This variant is more dangerous.
"Baba, can you get the vaccine?"
There's not enough for everyone
long lines at the hospitals
"Okay, hang in there. Please don't leave home
now."

The cases are rising, our neighbor uncle, his
daughter,
the old shopkeeper, the plumber, Raju, Baba's
friend…
All sick
Bodies piling up like leaves in autumn
Yellow, dry, wilted.
Only more putrid smelling, engulfing
neighborhoods
"Please don't leave home now."

This variant is more dangerous
not enough hospital beds for everyone
long wait-times for the vaccine.
Your grandmother is sick,
and your uncle
only forty-five, young and exuberant
"Please don't leave home now."

Two family members, gone.

On arrival

Two years later . . .

Landed at the airport.
The air is painfully humid
the spices have lost their aroma
the chai, as cold as an uninterested lover
a long and arduous sickness
and two years of neglect.

My big Shah Rukh Khan poster looks faded
dust, part sunlight from the west-side window
my room has empty cobwebs
perhaps the spiders have abandoned us.
A long and arduous sickness
and two years of neglect.

My parents have aged
as if by almost seven years
but it's only been two!
Their wrinkles, the faint cracks in the walls
that old beehive in our curry tree
empty, dry, dangling alone in exhaustion.

I gather my broken pieces together
I have aged too
as if by almost seven years
but it's only been two.

Where are you from?

They ask me, "So, where are you from?"
How do I say the name of one place when I
belong to so many?
Should I tell them where I was born or
should I say the names of all the places
we moved to as a family of four tagging along
with my father,
our sole breadwinner.
Should I tell them about the new home I made in
another country,
when I was in my twenties because that was
where I belonged,
or should I tell them about the place where my
daughter was born,
and I made a new home out of her first cries.
What if I have many homes and each home is a
vessel
containing the magic dust of memories lost and
found.

Kalbaisakhi

Monsoon arrives holding Kalbaisakhi's hand
Kalbaisakhi; a nor'wester brings
thunder and rain and
a much needed respite after
savage summer scorched its way
through homes, schools, fields, farms, ponds,
and rivers.

It seeped through me with an intensity
that left me parched while the sweat beads
trickled down my body
like soldiers exhausted from fighting the heat.

Every year
I wait for you, dear Kalbaisakhi.
You rummage and ruffle everything
with a childlike excitement that is both
joyous and terrifying.

I will pick up the broken pieces tomorrow
like I always have.

Lovers in the kitchen

Amid the dance of aromas
in a kitchen adorned with cumin's warmth
and the embrace of cloves and nutmeg
a romance unfolds
between two people who have nothing in
common
other than their love for food.

A love story laced with the secrets of turmeric
fragrant memories of saffron and ginger
and a little tease of paprika
Perhaps the lovers will make be a dish to
remember
make a symphony of spices rare
a new flavorful pair.

Puddles of delight

Waterlogged streets in my neighborhood
weave stories untold
and I scream at them, "I don't live here
anymore!"
In the downpour's rhythm, a home I had once
known
has now become distant like an old garment
that fits no more.

Long ago, I splashed through these puddles
with my childhood's delight,
floating paper boats till they went out of sight.
The croaking orchestra of frogs
under muted streetlights
through rain-kissed whispers and confessions
untold
I also sailed away carrying memories dusty and
old.

Old and new

Crossed the border of familiarity
with old habits,
and entered new ones.
Lost memories of old friends who
once were sources of comfort,
confidants who guarded my darkest secrets.
I crossed the border of old reassurances,
and entered new ones.
The new relations are more fleeting.
Their reassurances are casual.
Their comforts are temporary and
their pace noncommittal.
Yet in the absence of long-term security,
I find freedom.
Freedom from promises that I don't need to
fulfill.
I crossed the border of old commitments
and new commitments, I shall make no more.

Smelling sexy

Doesn't the kitchen smell sexy?
Warm, spicy and luxurious,
especially on days when leftovers are plenty
and the vegetables look plump and fresh.
The apples may have an extra blush on their
cheeks,
the rice whiter and fluffier than most days.
Your salad with a special crunch
gently seduces you to touch, feel, and consume.
The kitchen smells sexy when it is plentiful
in its youthful power to satiate
the stomach, mind and soul.

Our terrace garden

21

Reds, pinks, yellows and blues
in every corner, in every hue
our terrace garden blooms and blossoms
with dahlias, gardenias, petunias, and lilies
egg plants, okras, and red, hot chilies
and there is a corner where I often rest
I undress my mind taking it off anxiety's crest
our terrace garden complies and guards it till
daybreak
till the dahlias have spent all their sun rays on
me
I collect my bare mind as if to see
embalmed in silent whispers
and droplets of dew
the flowers in my terrace garden
fill me with hopes anew.

www.ingramcontent.com/pod-product-compliance
Lightning Source LLC
LaVergne TN
LVHW010905200726

843508LV00012B/2984